BREATHE
AN ANXIETY MEMOIR

BREATHE

AN ANXIETY MEMOIR

Alivia Jones

CONFESSIONS
PUBLISHING

Scripture quotations marked (ESV) are taken from the *Holy Bible*, English Standard Version © 2001 by Crossway Bibles, a division of Good News Publishers. Used by permission. All rights reserved.

Scripture quotations marked (NIV) are taken from the *Holy Bible*, New International Version. Zondervan Publishing House © 1984. Used by permission. All rights reserved.

Scripture quotations marked (NLT) are taken from the *Holy Bible*, New Living Translation © 2004. Wheaton, III: Tyndale House Publisher.

Breathe: An Anxiety Memoir

Copyright © 2021 Alivia Jones

ISBN: 978-1-7359620-4-7

Printed and bound in the United States of America.

All rights reserved. No part of this book may be reproduced, stored in a retrieval system, or transmitted in any form or by any means, electronic, mechanical, photocopying, recording, or otherwise without written permission of the author, Alivia Jones.

Editor: Janet Amann and Analise Jones

Cover Design: Alivia Jones

CONFESSIONS
PUBLISHING

Confessions Publishing is a subsidiary of Roszien Kay LLC, Lancaster, CA 93536.

For information regarding discounts on bulk purchase and all other inquiries please contact the author directly at authoralivia@gmail.com.

For My Mom,
You're so brave.
I love you.

ACKNOWLEDGMENT

—— ❧ ——

I want to thank every single person who has helped me through this difficult, challenging, and exigent time in my life.

My wonderful family: Krystal, Tom, Analise, Sam, and Daisy.

My grandparents: Ama and Pa

My editor, Janet.

My best friend, Abigail.

My amazing counselors & those who have supported me throughout my journey. I love each one of you who has helped me to make this book possible. I am blessed to have those who have helped me grow in God's love, and help me grow stronger through him.

CONTENTS

PROLOGUE

~~

To be honest I never saw myself writing an autobiography. Anxiety is a personal thing and I was not sure if I was ready to announce my disorder to the world. It was my mom, Krystal, who had the idea for me to write an anxiety memoir. I didn't know what to write about, so she suggested I write a memoir about my life with anxiety.

At first, I wasn't too thrilled with the idea. I worried about what people might think of me and how they would look at me. But then I realized that I am not the only one dealing with anxiety. I realized that I would be an encouragement to others by writing my story. It would give those reading something to put their faith in by looking at someone else's perspective. I will tell you though, none of this was easy.

It was a long, exhausting, and stressful process. I spent a lot of time rethinking writing this book. But, I pushed myself through it and here I am. This is my story . . .

CHAPTER 1:
JUST ANOTHER PANIC ATTACK

"If you can't fly then run, if you can't run then walk, if you can't walk then crawl, but whatever you do you have to keep moving forward."

(Martin Luther King Jr.)

My heart is racing. My chest feels so tight that I can barely breathe. My stomach is twisting in pain. I think I am going to be sick. I feel lightheaded; like I might collapse at any moment. The room is spinning, making it almost impossible to see what's in front of me. My heart rate climbs by the second.

Thump, thump, thump.

I am panting now. My lungs feel like they are about to explode.

Thump, thump, thump.

"Ughhh. Ughhh. Ughhh!" I groan in agony. I want it to stop!

I sink to the ground, crying, as everything worsens by the second.

I focus on my breathing.

In. One, two, three.

Out. One, two, three.

My heart slows; it's pace lessening. My stomach calms, and my head stops spinning. I continue to take deep, calming breaths, allowing my mind to wander away from the future, and back into the present. I sigh in relief. Everything is okay now, just another panic attack.

CHAPTER 2:
ANXIETY DOES NOT OWN YOU

"Sometimes the bad things that happen in our lives put us directly on the path to the most wonderful things that will ever happen to us."

(Nicole Reed)

L isten to me when I say anxiety does not own you. Anxiety is fake. It's not real. It's like a little fantasy troll sitting around in your mind, telling you stupid lies because it has nothing better to do.

During a panic attack, my amygdala is setting off a fake alarm in my body telling me something that is not going to happen, causing me to be focused on the future and not now. So, how exactly do you get rid of this annoying little pest of a thing?

To do this, I use my strategies to overcome it. It may sound impossible, but even though it may prove to be difficult at times, it will be worth it.

Start by drawing out your enemy (aka anxiety). Make it look like something silly that you can easily scare away. Color it in with your favorite color. Frame it, and hang it on your wall to remind you that anxiety is defeatable.

Next, write some inspirational quotes on paper and hang them on your wall. Things like "Anxiety cannot win", and "You are stronger than anxiety." Get creative. This can be used as a distraction as well as an encouragement when you feel anxiety settling in.

One of the best things you can do is exercise daily. It has been scientifically proven to help with anxiety and as a bonus, it can help you to stay fit. There are other activities you can do to help you to cope with anxiety. I tried to meditate, but I lost interest as well as time.

A method I stumbled upon on the Internet has proven helpful as well. This method is called grounding. To "ground" you take time to look around you. Name five things you can see, four things you can touch, three things you can hear, two things you can smell, and one thing you can taste. This allows you to be aware of your surroundings and can hopefully help you to push that anxiety troll out.

Practice your breathing, too. Close your eyes. Count to ten. Focus on the now.

Aside from breathing, try to find a coping skill. I know how hard it can be to try and find a good coping skill that works for you. Honestly it might take some time. Even though this may be the case, don't give up. I didn't. Because I didn't, I found how much pets can help. In fact, my pets have helped me a lot.

CHAPTER 3:
EMOTIONAL SUPPORT

———— ∿ ————

"The companionship of an animal can offer comfort, help ease anxiety, and build self-confidence for people anxious about going out into the world. Because pets live in the moment—they don't worry about what happened yesterday or what might happen tomorrow—they can help you become more mindful and appreciate the joy of the present."

(Lawrence Robinson and Jeanne Segal)

I want to take a minute to tell you about my zoo of emotional support animals. We have a variety of fuzzy, sweet, and cute pets. I will start with our dogs. We brought Kipper into our family when I was around seven years old. He struggles with major anxiety issues that I can relate to. He is a black and brown Cocker Spaniel-Cavalier.

We got our second dog when I was 10 years old. Mya is the sweetest big baby; ginger and white American Bulldog-Boxer mix. When I have a panic attack, she butts me with her head, licks my hand, and barks. She does a great job of distracting me when I am mad, nervous, or scared. She distracts me from saying mean things, having a panic attack, and from whatever it is that's scaring me.

We also have nine cats. Yes, you heard me correctly, we have nine cats. Malkey, Sophie, and Lucy have been with us as long as I can remember. Then, last year we ended up losing Sophie at the age of 16. It was a difficult time for all of us, especially my sister Analise. She had gotten her when they were both babies.

Analise was allowed to get a kitten to help cope with the loss. She picked out a long hair Dilute Calico from the shelter. We had to go back three times before she reached the weight requirements; and before we were allowed to adopt her. Analise named her Kyla and gave her Sophie's middle name, Maria.

We soon decided to get a friend for Kyla and my mom. She was a black and orange Calico named Sunshine. Well, of course, we could not stop there, so my mom and Analise went and adopted a black kitten as a surprise for my other sister, Daisy. It was her birthday and Daisy named her Vampirina.

Around this same time, Sunshine got ill and we had to put her down. She had a rare kitten disease that was slowly killing her. This was again really hard for all of us.

My mom then adopted another kitten to help with the loss of Sunshine. She and Analise again went and got a surprise kitten. His name is Ludo. Now, this kitten has a million nicknames like Squishy, Squishum, Cookie, BooBoo, etc. My mom ended up falling in love with another kitten shortly after we adopted Ludo. Her name is Remi. Then, we rescued our last one; Dosa.

I don't even know how people know what cats we are talking about, we have so many. Well, there are seven and somehow we made it to nine. After a family member's death, we inherited her two cats, Tutti and Jenny. Jenny is small, black, white, and blind. Then, Tutti is a Tabico meaning she is a Tabby Calico. She has a humongous belly!

My cats make me laugh when I am nervous, smile when I am sad, and happy when I am mad. Their weight on my stomach comforts me and their soft fur helps to calm me in any situation. Ludo and Remi will even lick me when I am feeling sad. Our cats have helped me a lot when it comes to my anxiety.

Cats and dogs aren't our only pets. We also have rats. Yes, rats. We have cats and rats in the same house. I wanted a pet to try and ease my anxiety, so I adopted three baby rats. They were five months old at the time. Batgirl is a black Berkshire rat. Posey has Oreo markings and Piper is a hooded grey and white rat.

They are stinky, messy, and loud! Yet, somehow they make up for it in cuteness. They are pretty lively, so it is difficult to cuddle them, but their constant mischievous running around helps distract me when an attack is coming on. They are about two years old now and do a great job as my emotional support rats.

Our last pets are fish. We have a 200-gallon tank, and living in it are four Oscars and one Plecosomous. If you don't know what an Oscar is, they are giant fish that come in a few different colors. Right now they are still young, so they are only about eight or nine inches. Sometimes, I like to just stare into the tank and watch them swim around when I feel an attack coming on.

All of our pets have helped me with my anxiety and sensory issues.

CHAPTER 4:

FLASHBACK— MOM'S P.O.V

"By being yourself, you put something wonderful in the world that was not there before."

(Edwin Elliot)

Alivia has always dealt with different sensory issues that interfere with normal coping skills. They add another stressful element to her already stressed out brain; interfering with the calming messages she tries to send herself by irritating her with their annoyances . . . scratchy fabrics, tight clothing squeezing in on her, puffy coats, shirt and pant seams, sock seams, sock bands, zippers, tangly hair that has to be brushed.

ALIVIA JONES

Alivia is also annoyed when it's too hot, too cold, too loud, too quiet, too many noises, too many people talking, too much laughter, too windy, too sweaty, too much chatter, too many people too close. As well as when there are crowds, pushing, shoving, breathing on her … the list goes on and on.

These annoyances challenge her daily to cope with life. They interfere with her ability to process things as you and I would. As well as her ability to tune it out, ignore it, walk away, or adjust to it. She shuts down. She screams. She cries. She melts down. It overwhelms her.

From the time she was just an infant, she hated being touched or held by anyone. I could cuddle her for a short time while feeding her, but she would rather be lying down, snuggling with her baby blankies—Pinky and Purpily.

I was always worried she wasn't warm enough. I couldn't swaddle her . . . according to her it was always too tight. I couldn't put her in warm footsies . . . she felt they were too hot. I needed something just right. So, I happened to find these lightly knit blankies at a second-hand store (which started a craze of having to search out more, but that's another story). The blankies were light enough that I could cover her with them and they worked . . . no more screaming fits. No more worrying if she was warm enough. They also became her comfort and still are today. They were her first anxiety coping mechanisms.

CHAPTER 5:
MOM'S P.O.V
SOMETHING'S NOT RIGHT

"What seem to us as bitter trials are often blessings in disguise."
(Oscar Wilde)

As she grew out of her baby stage into her toddler stage, I started to notice additional signs that something was not quite right. She had a very short temper. When she got angry she would throw herself into walls and spin in circles over and over to calm herself.

When running errands, she did not want to hold hands or stay with me. She had no fear of danger. She would run away from me in parking lots and hide in stores; I had to put her on a child's leash.

I also noticed she was a late talker. Alivia started talking at three, which threw her communication skills off, making her even more frustrated than she was before. She could not explain her frustrations or express her feelings. She could be happy safely exploring in her house or playing alone, but if things changed she couldn't handle it.

Her fearless personality got her into some trouble as well. Often it seemed she would laugh in danger's face. When she was just two years old, she climbed up on a bunch of moving boxes giggling and thought she was hilarious. Luckily fearing she'd fall and hurt herself, I stopped her before she got hurt.

Going to parks or just playing outside, she had to be watched very closely. She would run down steep slides without fear or try to jump off play structures, rocks, etc. She was exhausted and so different from her older sister; but she did like her quiet space and was content to be left alone to nap and have quiet time.

When Alivia was about three I knew in my gut something was off, she was recommended to get tested through Kaiser's Autism Center. There were two very nice, young girls doing the testing. One with blond hair, the other with brown. Alivia went with them, happily. She played a few fun games with them for the testing, and they challenged her social cues.

Soon after, we received results stating that she had High-Functioning Asperger's Syndrome. This made sense of the sensory issues, fearlessness, need for quiet, not wanting to be held, fear of strangers, the anger of schedule changes and surprises, lack of communication, and expressive language. It would soon also give understanding to her lack of deciphering social cues and fear of social situations—aka school.

CHAPTER 6:
MOM'S P.O.V SOCIAL ANXIETY

"When you're feeling anxious, remember that you're still you. You are not anxiety. Whenever you feel otherwise, remember that's just the anxiety talking. You are still you and hold the power in every moment."

(Deanne Repich)

After the diagnosis, she started speech and preschool. She was not a fan! The speech teacher she liked but hated being challenged and motivations did not work for her as easily as they did for other kids.

Leaving her at preschool was heartbreaking. She would stand by the fence, crying as I drove away day after day. She only had to stay for a couple of hours, but imagine having to leave your little girl who you know struggles so much with the fear of the unknown in a place. She didn't feel safe. I knew it was because she didn't trust them yet . . . Unfortunately, as time went on she never did grow to trust. As a result, she cried every day.

We tried two different preschools. But both schools had little girls who were mean to her and tormented her daily, making her even more afraid to go to school. Some of the fear came from just not being able to understand other kids. Socially she struggled with communication and she never liked playing in groups . . . kids are unpredictable, so she chose to hang out with a teacher or sit alone.

When I would come to pick her up at the end of the couple hours, I would find her alone sitting in the classroom, or not playing on the playground. I could only imagine how lonely she felt.

In kindergarten Alivia had a very sweet teacher, who she enjoyed. She also made her first friend. That year went pretty well. I volunteered in the class a lot and her new friend was shy, so they got along really well. The teacher had a soft demeanor and was so kind.

She had the same experience in first grade. However, timed tests started in first grade and added a new fear . . . the fear of not getting things right . . . the fear of not finishing and being timed . . .time ticking away and distracting her from doing the work. She would cry and hide under the table, refusing to do them.

Then came second grade. She still hated school and would cling to me every morning, not wanting to go inside the classroom. I would have to pull her off of me and force her to go, handing her off to her teacher and closing a door on her as I walked away, again, torturing a mother's heart.

Her friend was in a different second grade class, and that saddened her because she was like a security blanket to her. This is when I'd say Alivia's social anxiety crept up on her and was finally evident. It caused her to be silent. It caused her to shut down. She started hiding under desks and throwing fits in class. She even cursed out at her teacher in anger. When I would come to pick her up, she was always mentally and emotionally exhausted from trying to hold it together all day.

What they saw at school of her trying to cope with a day was nothing close to what an actual meltdown looked like at home. The afternoons were filled with major tantrums, meltdowns, screaming fits, rage, and anger. She wasn't getting schoolwork done in class, so it was all being sent home for me to do with her. Along with the already given homework, but, unlike the teacher, I was now trying to accomplish this with her emotional state of being exhausted. The mix of this was like trying to help a tornado do school work. The spiral out of control from her anxiety made a very unenjoyable time. That's when I decided to homeschool her.

CHAPTER 7:
HOMESCHOOL

〰️

"Worry is like a rocking chair: it gives you something to do but never gets you anywhere."

(Erma Bombeck)

Homeschooling has helped me in so many wonderful ways. Being homeschooled is beneficial because I don't have to worry about being around all the drama, social obstacles, and other anxiety-provoking things. The bullying, fights, smoking, vaping, alcohol, threats, cheating, teasing . . . and the list just goes on.

Luckily for me, my mom was a teacher for a few years before my sister and I were born. But when we were born she became a devoted stay at home mom. That is one of the hardest jobs in the world I think. Any job with kids is!

When my mom realized that public school was not for me and chose to homeschool me, I did not yet realize the privilege I was being given. I'm sure I was happy since I was a shy girl, but I never really thought of it as something I should be thanking her for until around middle school.

It wasn't until I discovered that so many of my friends wanted to be homeschooled, and could not due to their mom and dad's work schedule that I became thankful. I discovered that what I had was a huge act of grace; a wonderful gift that I did not deserve.

I'm extremely thankful to my mom for being the best homeschool teacher in the world (thank you mom!) I know that being homeschooled is a privilege that not everyone gets, and that makes it even more special.

CHAPTER 8:
IN COME'S KATIE

～

"Today's a perfect day for a whole new start. Let go of fear and free your mind. It's time to open your heart."

(Chris Butler)

I hated getting things wrong, and I got mad when I did things wrong. That is one of the reasons school was such a struggle for me. We started attending a Charter School when I was in 6th grade, and that's when my mom sought help for me with my homework.

My tutor's name was Katie; she tutored me 7th grade through 9th grade and was a huge part of my life. Katie is a mid-thirties, feisty, sweet woman who pushed me to reach my goals. After just a few months of tutoring with her, I started doing much, much better in school. I was not having as many meltdowns, if any, and when I did get a problem wrong it was easier for me to correct it without hinting at anger inside. I just want to thank Ms. Katie for pushing me beyond my measures, being there for me, and loving me the past couple of years of my life.

CHAPTER 9:
KATIE'S P.O.V

"Once you choose hope, anything is possible."
(Christopher Reeve)

Alivia is happy, carefree, friendly, funny, easy to get along with, open-minded, willing to listen, a pleasure to be around, grateful, honest, and willing to learn when she is not anxious. She is great, amazing, and wonderful.

Alivia is at her highest potential when anxiety is not roaming around her. I can tell when she is anxious because she becomes impatient and irritable. Causing her to disengage, become reserved, and quiet. When this happens it's a sign that she is no longer hearing what she wants to hear. She then does not understand things which cause her to believe those around her are being unfair.

When you are experiencing anxiety, it's like you are trapped in your head. It feels like you are drowning, or even choking metaphorically, like the world is caving in on you. Everything feels stressful and heavy.

It is very hard to see the possibility of a positive outcome. You worry all the time about what might, could, or should happen. Or what didn't happen, won't happen, or what did happen. Your thoughts are racing, and you cannot find the brakes. You second guess yourself, and everyone else. Your judgment is clouded, you can't think clearly or rationally. It feels like if something bad could happen it will happen.

To overcome anxiety, you must be willing to overcome it. I think faith has a lot to do with it if you allow it (faith) to be bigger than your fears. It is important to talk about your anxiety and not let it be something you are ashamed of. So that you can realize you are not as alone as you may think. Seek help from family, friends, and experts.

I suffer from anxiety myself, so I can understand how frustrating and debilitating it can be. I understand that there are times when you feel like you can't control it because it is controlling you. There are probably multiple other people in your life who can relate as well, you just don't know it yet.

Alivia,

When you tell your story that is a powerful thing to do because it empowers you as well as the people you share it with. The people who love you, love you even when you are anxious. We only want to help you feel your best. Remember that it is okay to ask for help.

Alivia, my love, even when life seems scary, dark, and lonely, please remember that happiness can be found even in the darkest times if you only remember to turn on the light. Always seek the light. When it is hard to find, remember that the light resides in you.

Katie

CHAPTER 10:
HOLLIE'S P.O.V

"Courage doesn't always roar. Sometimes courage is the quiet voice at the end of the day saying, 'I will try again tomorrow.'"

(Mary Ann Radmacher)

Sometimes, when you have known a person for a certain amount of time you forget how you met them. For me, I remember first meeting Alivia when she was on a walk with her family at my house. She was a very different person then. Because she was so different, I got to know her so slowly that I only know who she is now.

I know Alivia for being a relaxed, engaging, and fun girl who always cheers me up with a big hug or smile; in the same way, I always try to do the same for her when she looks worried or upset.

When Alivia is not nervous she can focus and get a lot done. She can find projects to do and ideas to work on. She loves to chat. It helps her get her mind off what she's worried about and makes it easier to go into the situations she may be worried about.

Those situations usually are something new, something different. When she is starting to panic it's because it's a new thing to her, something different coming up in her life. She loses the sparkle in her eye and tends to get quiet. When this happens I know she is in the midst of panic. As the panic attack hits her, she gets frazzled and it's difficult for her to think rationally about things. She gets angry and ignores people's advice when in this state of panic.

When you live with anxiety it's just a crippling experience to have to live with everyday. Anxiety alters the decisions you make and your priorities get jumbled, causing you to unsee the positive perspective on new, scary situations.

I believe Alivia can overcome her anxiety with lots of cognitive practice. She can practice being in difficult, anxiety-provoking situations and overcoming her fears and anxieties. If she focuses on her relationship with God and surrounds herself with those who love her she can live in a happier state. Considering she takes care of herself and makes sure her body and brain are regulated with exercise, diet, sleep, vitamins, and medication.

Alivia,

I admire you for the passion you have in life. I admire that even if things are difficult, you come around eventually. You don't let depression and anxiety get the better of you. Instead, you take these imperfections and learn to grow with them.

You are good at analyzing yourself. I hope that gift helps you be open to what areas you want to work on and change, and what areas God has gifted you in.

It has been fun to see you grow and mature for the past couple of years. I have enjoyed being a part of your life for the past few years. You never fail to make me smile and I look forward to seeing you. You are a kind-hearted young woman and I love how you dream. Keep being transparent, Alivia.

I know that it puts you in socially vulnerable places when others know how you feel; but as you get older others will be refreshed by being around someone who doesn't hide who they are.

You are a gift to anyone that God puts in your life. Keep shining bright and asking God to guide you along the way.

"For God has not given us a spirit of fear and timidity, but of power, love, and self-discipline."

(2 Timothy 1:7 NLT)

Hollie

CHAPTER 11:
HIGH SCHOOL

"This is a new year. A new beginning. And things will change."

(Taylor Swift)

I remember the day eighth grade ended, that dreaded feeling crept over me like a dark cloud. Even though the ninth grade was still two months away, I couldn't relax. I was so afraid of the unknown, that I kept obsessing over the matter that was still so far into the future.

Every fun event could not be enjoyed. I threw up over everything and anything because I knew exactly what was coming. High School, it scared me. As each week crept away from me, I felt even more anxious. First, it was three weeks, then two, then one. Before I knew it, it was the morning of my very first day, and boy was I nervous!

I do not remember much about that day, honestly, but I'll try my best to explain it. I didn't eat, which was no surprise, and then before I knew it I was off to school. Around that time, my sister had just recently gotten her license. This meant that I'd be going with her, instead of my mom. That made me even more worried, so there I was, heading to my first period— Algebra 1. I opened the door and was greeted by my teacher. She was very energetic and seemed nice.

I spotted a girl from my class the year before and took a seat by her. We talked for a little while, and then she introduced me to her friends. That's when I met Abigail, soon enough, we were best friends. One of the first real best friends I've had. I'm certain without her, I'd be eating lunch by myself and probably still dreading going to school.

Abby is an amazing friend; she's always there for me, whether I'm struggling with school, depression, or anxiety. I'm so thankful for her being there for me through all this, and always cheering me up with a hug or smile. Abigail is so wonderful and I thank God for putting her in my life. I could not have asked for a better best friend.

Despite the fact that I had a best friend to help me to make the transition, that first semester was rough. I dropped English and started taking the online course a few weeks into the school year. The homework was rough, and I wasn't very motivated to get it done.

At the end of my first semester of highschool, I had two C's, one B, and three A's. I was disappointed in myself for having such low grades, but it motivated me to try harder the next semester. Before semester two began, I made myself a promise that I would end Biology with an A, and because I pushed myself I did.

When you try your best, you succeed. I had to remind myself of this. I had to tell myself "as long as I am willing to try my best I will succeed."

CHAPTER 12:
MOM'S P.O.V —ALIVIA'S HIGH SCHOOL TRANSITION

"You've been doing a great job considering all you've been up against."

(Unknown)

High School. All the fear of the unknown; not knowing what it would be like began another new battle with her anxiety and later dark thoughts that affected her self confidence and worth on this earth. It is a constant battle as I walk alongside her on this journey . . . knowing when to push her and challenge her and knowing when to just be there. It is trying to know when to reach out for help from her counselors when I cannot do it anymore. It is knowing her well enough to know when things are getting too overwhelming. It is facing the hard reality that what she's struggling with can't be fixed by me or a doctor; and that sometimes my only hope is prayers to God.

Medication, doctors, psychologists, counselors, unconditional love, and support only go so far . . . when you have to watch your child battle the darkness of depression and even contemplate her worth on this earth, it is a huge punch to the gut and heart. It's not a feeling I'd wish on anyone, but I know God has big plans for my girl!

She has been through so much and I know her journey has only begun. I pray every day her struggles push her to have confidence in herself and God. I try to teach her to stand up for herself and be an advocate for herself and others.

I often tell Alivia: "*never let anyone put a label on you! Never let anyone ever dictate how you feel about yourself, especially if it makes you feel like crap! You're in charge of you!*"

God made you perfectly as seen in His eyes! You might not believe that sometimes, but remember to take a deep breath. God is in control and He'll get you through whatever you're going through.

So . . . Calm down. Just breathe. It's going to be okay."

Cast all your anxiety on him because he cares for you (1 Peter 5:7 NIV).

CHAPTER 13:
ABIGAIL'S P.O.V

"A friend is one who overlooks your broken fence and admires the flowers in your garden."

(Unknown)

Alivia is a very joyful and funny person. She laughs at the most random of things, and she tells me the most random, but funny jokes. I can always count on her to be there for me and make me laugh when I'm not feeling my best.

I can tell when she's starting to panic because she starts getting shaky, and uneasy mentally. I can just tell that she is not feeling great, and a panic attack is on its way. She starts looking extremely pissed and starts sighing at everything the teacher says and acts like everything they are saying is too complicated. She just has a sense of defeat shining down on her.

When she has a panic attack, I get stressed, because I'm worried about her. I don't want Alivia to feel like that; it just makes me sad to see her like that.

Her panic attacks usually last around 10 minutes. When Alivia is in the middle of one, she seems to just give up and give in, telling herself what the voices inside want her to believe. It is very sad to watch her suffer like this. If I could, I would just crawl inside and bring a sword with me, so that I can just chop up all those little people and defeat their voices.

I try my best to be there for her during a panic attack. I'm just there for her. I reassure her, with the fact that I am there, and that everything will be okay. I comfort her.

I think anyone can overcome it by trying to tune out the voices in their heads—the ones that tell you that you are not good enough. The voices that tell you it is too hard or you can not do it (by the way these are very common lies and misconceptions).

You can do it because you've done it before and you can do it again.

Anxiety is different for everyone. I think that living with it is very, very stressful. Because you don't know what's going to happen; and every situation that you have been through is different from each other.

Alivia,

I hope I can be a place where you come and don't feel stressed. I want you to trust me and be okay with who you are. And who you will become without looking at yourself with negative eyes like the ones that judge you often. You are loved.

Abigail

CHAPTER 14:
BREATHE, YOU'RE OKAY

———— ❧ ————

"Don't assume I'm weak because I have panic attacks. You'll never know the amount of strength it takes to face the world every day."

(Unknown)

I am in Math class, and everything around me is too much to handle right now. The teacher's voice is blaring in my ears, everyone around me is moving around, asking questions. It is so much louder to me than it really is. My vision is blurring quickly, and I feel like any second I might burst out in tears.

Markers squeaking on the whiteboard. Ugh. It makes me wince just thinking of it.

I want to raise my hand, and hide out in the bathroom, but then I think, "I am much stronger than that. I can do this."

It worsens. Classmates are yelling, music playing, chairs squeaking, and the click-clack of laptop keys.

I breathe.

In. Out.

In. Out.

That's it. Keep breathing.

In. Out.

In. Out.

I'm okay.

"No, you're not. Listen to all the noise. Doesn't that bother you?"

The sounds come streaming in, and I cannot seem to shut them out.

"See, you're not okay. You're panicking."

No! I am okay. I am okay. I am okay.

The voices in my head beg to differ. *"Listen to me. You will never be okay. Anxiety haunts you. It will never go away. It's your boss. I am the boss of you. Hear that? That's the truth."*

I close my eyes, breathing deeply still, aiming my focus away from the pestering voices. You are okay.

"Are you, though?"

I am okay.

"You're never going to be okay."

I am okay, and I'm not listening to you! Hear that?

Silence.

I am okay.

CHAPTER 15:
THE LONELY SEA
OF DEPRESSION

*"The only thing more exhausting than being depressed is
pretending that you're not."*

(Anonymous)

I first started noticing the way my mood changed when I was thirteen years old. I know I was at that age and all, but this was something different, something awful.

Everybody knows the simple feelings, happy and sad. Happy is full of smiles, joy, and hugs. It's what everyone wants to feel. Sad on the other hand is gloomy, bleak, and disgusting. Nobody wants to feel that way.

Unfortunately, that's how I was feeling. Gloomy, bleak, and disgusting. I was feeling sad. I was in the dark.

"The broken will always be able to love harder than most because once you've been in the dark, you learn to appreciate everything that shines."

(Anonymous)

At the age of thirteen, I found myself in the dark a lot. I went in and out of depression. One day I'd feel like I'd want to jump up and celebrate. And the very next I'd feel like a truckload of boulders was dumped on top of me.

The happiness would come for a short visit, maybe a couple of days, but then the dark would take over, crashing down on me like a giant wave. This wave would take a stronghold on me and pull me back out into the lonely sea of depression.

CHAPTER 16:
THE STORM

~

"No storm, not even the one in your life, can last forever. The storm is just passing over."

(Iyanla Vanzant)

There was a boat in the middle of the ocean. This was no ordinary boat, though. Aboard it was a girl. A very brave girl who had been in this same boat, in the same place for quite a while now.

She had thought of jumping overboard into the wrestling waves many times now. She had thought of giving up way too much. She had thought she was not fit to live in this world anymore. She wanted to forget about her pain and sorrow. She wanted to be happy, but she didn't know how. However much she tried, however hard she tried, she always ended up back in the same boat, in the same sea of depression.

During my freshman year of high school, I went in and out of depression so much I didn't even know whether or not I was just sad or depressed. *"Do not get lost in a sea of despair. Do not become bitter or hostile. Be hopeful, be optimist*ic," is what I kept telling myself.

My depression hurt me in a way nothing has ever before. It stung my heart and ripped me away from my happiness so that the only thing left was the depressed, icky feeling.

In December of 2019, I all of a sudden found myself amid a horrible case of depression. I avoided my friends and my family whenever I could. I didn't want them to see me like that. I was in an awful state and I didn't know when I would come out of it. Honestly, I didn't think I would.

On December 15th, 2019 I started praying for God to take my life. I thought my life was ready to be over. I didn't think there was a point to living it to it's full. I was exhausted and very done.

God didn't answer my prayers right away, though. I kept on praying every night in tears for him to not let me wake up the next morning. I didn't want to wake up and find myself in the same situation. I wanted to die and have God take me home to Heaven.

Heaven was supposed to be perfect. There was happiness there; and that's what I wanted, happiness.

I waited for a few days for God to take my life and bring me home, but that didn't happen. By then, I was so very depressed that I decided the only way to get rid of my hurting was to die. I already knew that God wasn't going to take my life, so I told myself that I was done waiting. It was time to take matters into my own hands.

Suicidal thoughts started bouncing around in my head on December 19th, 2019.

Nobody cares about you. They won't care if you're gone.

Kill yourself already.

Your life is over.

Die. Die. Die.

I want to be dead.

Just do it already.

On December 21st I shut myself in my bathroom and knelt to the floor. I allowed myself to cry for a long time.

Then, I prayed. "God, I'm hurting." I said, "I don't know what to do anymore. I need to go home now."

With that, I stood up, shaking with every step, and looked myself over in the mirror. I told myself "'You can do this. It'll be over soon." Then I stopped. "Am I crazy?", I thought to myself, "Am I really about to do this?"

Then I knew. I couldn't bring myself to commit suicide no matter how hard I tried. God wouldn't let me.

CHAPTER 17:
IT'S FOR MY GOOD

"Love your future more than your past"

(Joe Despenz)

I don't know what it was that stopped me from committing suicide that day. I just remember wiping my tears from my cheeks and walking out of the bathroom, not giving it another thought.

All I know is that it was all part of God's plan for me to be there, happy again, with my family on Christmas Day.

In the second semester of my freshman year, I was doing much better mentally. Mostly because I had started taking what I call my "happy pills." My psychiatrist prescribed me medication shortly after my suicide attempt. She told my mom many things about my depression and suicidal thoughts.

"Don't leave her home alone."

"Don't let her be alone on the internet."

"Watch and note her mood."

I felt like I was in prison. Everyone else my age got to stay home alone. Everyone else my age had a phone and always asked why I didn't. I felt I was being treated like a baby, but I knew it was all for the best.

CHAPTER 18:
THE NIGHTMARE

"Love and kindness are never wasted. They always make a difference. They bless the one who receives them, and they bless you, the giver."

(Barbara De Angelis)

So, in the second semester of freshman year, I was doing way better. No suicidal thoughts, rare depressive moods. I was feeling great, until the fire went out and in came the nightmare.

You see, I wanted to forget about my suicide attempt. Pretend it didn't happen. But, certain people were making forgetting about it hard.

I was at school one day, minding my own business, when this boy comes up to me and mouths, "Kill yourself." It was obvious that his message was meant for me. But, I shook it off and finished my day. At home though, I started to rethink my suicide attempt. Why didn't I go through with it to the end? That question was left unanswered when I fell asleep from an exhausting day.

Eventually forgetting that boy's comment, I went along with my life, starting to feel better again, until nightmare number two came in. I've never done anything bad. Well, for the most part. I'd been a Christian most of my life and I had always gone to church to volunteer and praise God. One day though I was hanging out with an old friend and her boyfriend and they were like, "C'mon. Let's ditch. Nobody wants to sit through service for an hour."

I agreed, not giving my choice much thought, and went to grab my water bottle. Well, then I hear her boyfriend's voice calling my name, so I turn around and he goes, "Hey, do everyone a favor and kill yourself, would you?"

He starts laughing with his friend and I just turn and walk away. I was so hurt that day. I found my pastor and told him, almost in tears the whole story. He listened to me and thanked me for coming to him. Then I went home and told my mom in tears. I have to admit those suicidal thoughts came and went that day, but again they were ignored and tossed aside when I fell asleep from another exhausting day.

CHAPTER 19:
COUNSELING

"Not all wounds are visible."

(Unknown)

I'm very fortunate because I've had so many people in my life who have helped me to thrive even with anxiety. I started going to counseling when I was around nine years old. My counselor is very sweet, and I've enjoyed working with her. I have been seeing her for almost four and a half years.

The first few months were hard. I was scared to go and be left in the room alone with her, so my mom came with me. It still took me a while before I was comfortable with her and ready to start talking about my fears.

When I was younger I used to play with my counselor, dolls, puzzles, drawing, and games. Now that I'm older I sit in a comfy chair and give her a brief recap of the past few weeks. I tell her about times when I got angry, anxious, or upset. We talk over these scenarios and resolve them the best we can. She asks me how my medication is working and what I've been doing lately. I wouldn't say that I look forward to going, but I know it helps me and because of this, I continue to be as positive as I can about seeking help.

When I was a little over the age of eleven I started seeing a psychiatrist as well. She is the one who first put me on my meds. She's very nice and I have also enjoyed working with her. My mom and I both go in and sit on a couch and talk to her. I also give her a detailed recap of what's happened since I last saw her.

CHAPTER 20:
COUNSELOR'S P.O.V

"Don't judge others. You never know what battle they are facing."

(Unknown)

L ife with anxiety can be exhausting, especially when you're first encountering it, and you don't understand it yet, or know what your triggers are, or what your strategies are to manage it. It is surprisingly very manageable and typically as people get older they're much more familiar with how to handle it. Hopefully, when it's more intense it's just a nuisance, and when it's just a little bit something more quirky, people learn to live with it.

I think Alivia's has come a long way since I met her. In a few ways she's changed in terms of her mental health struggles; that has gotten much better. They are not as intense, most of the time. She has matured so much and taken ownership of her mental well being. She has been able to figure out what coping strategies work for her and this has made her anxiety more manageable for her.

I've taught Alivia a combination of mental strategies. For example, giving herself reality checks, and learning not to focus on the negative, but the positive. We also have worked on a lot of problem-solving skills to overcome difficult situations; strategies of distractions and healthy outlets.

I believe that her medicine has helped, but I also think her maturity has helped. I would say that before meds and before she had the ability to apply the mental strategies everything was just much more intense. Her anxiety was more intense, her emotions were so overwhelming, keeping her behaviors in check was extremely difficult for her because of her lack of control. After meds, those things have disappeared and other things that persist are just not as overwhelming and I feel she can manage them well now.

I believe that she can overcome anxiety by continuing to do what she is already doing. Always taking another look at her self-help strategies and adding on to them.

Alivia,

I want you to know how proud I am of you. You never stopped trying, never stopped reaching out. You are always honest and open about your struggles. That allows people to be in a position to be able to help you. I just appreciate you and your willingness to trust me to help you. I believe in you 100%!

To anyone who has any difficult mental health challenges, or any life circumstances that are challenging, I would hope you are reading Alivia's story and be inspired, to know that everything is going to be okay.

-Dr. Deb

CHAPTER 21:
IT TAKES WORK

~

"The highest reward for a man's toil is not what he gets for it,
but what he becomes by it."

(John Ruskin)

Right now, I am currently seeing a counselor, a therapist, a psychiatrist, and a school counselor. Each one of them is helping me so much, and I can't even explain how grateful I am for every one of them.

My therapist and I work on exercises; such as jumping jacks, heel raises, push-ups, and crunches. We work on mind and body games, such as bean bag tossing, swinging, and board games. She works with me on how to better handle anxiety-provoking situations. We talk about how I feel during a panic attack and why I feel that way. Then we resolve the situation the best that we can.

My psychiatrist and I work on a growth mindset, breathing, grounding, and what to do during a panic attack. Sometimes, we play a fun game or paint. I am still seeing Dr. Deb and my other psychiatrist on top of this.

CHAPTER 22:
MY GIFT FROM GOD

"Love yourself a little harder when life seems impossible."

(Unknown)

I don't know where I would be right now without my medicine; if I would even be alive. The meds have done miracles for me. I haven't always had the advantage of this miracle though. Before I was given my meds, my anxiety was a whole different story. I can't even imagine living without them right now.

Before my meds, one of the worst things that happened was the throwing up. I would make myself sick because of how anxious I was. I would make myself gag over and over until finally, I'd throw up. This happened for no apparent reason, in a grocery store, at a park, in my bed.

These puke attacks would just come out of nowhere. Sometimes, I wouldn't even be nervous. They'd happen just because. It was awful. I'd hover over the toilet or the sink, feeling sick to my stomach. I'd throw up over and over until all that was left was the acid in my stomach. It'd sting my throat coming up, and burn my tongue.

After one of these attacks, my throat would feel extremely tight, and I'd be starving, but I was afraid to eat. I'd constantly skip meals because I was scared of throwing up. Every time I would even glance at my plate of food, I would feel sick. I'd find myself getting angry over the littlest things and I'd have constant meltdowns, it was just really bad.

Something else that came along with the anxiety was my stomach. When I would get anxious, so would my tummy. It would hurt so bad, and make horrible sounds. It would get upset, and it would give me diarrhea. Anytime I got nervous, the upset stomach would come with it; wherever I was, whatever I was doing. I'd feel like I was about to poop my pants whenever I experienced an anxiety attack.

Anxiety for me seemed to be a lot like the flu. You get chills, sudden flashes of heat, and an upset stomach, along with the puke. Just a horrible experience to have to go through.

My medicine was a literal miracle. After I started taking them everything happened at a much lower extent. If I threw up, it was only once every few weeks. Now it's only 3 or 4 times a year, if even that. This sounds like a lot, but to me, it's like a grain of salt out of the whole jar; it's so little compared to before.

I only have anxiety once in a blue moon now, and it's not nearly as intense anymore. I am now able to go places and enjoy it. I am now able to travel long distances without having sudden panic attacks in the car.

Everything is now better, and it's all because of my medicine. It has helped me so much and it continues to. I don't get sick over anything, and I don't run away from my fears. I am much stronger now, and much more fun to be around. I'm a miracle and a gift from God, just like my medication was to me.

CHAPTER 23:
FEAR

"Courage is not the absence of fear, but rather the judgment that something else is more important than fear."

(Ambrose Redmoon)

Another thing that came along with my anxious body was fear. Fear of what, you might ask? Everything and anything. I was scared of everything. What could happen to me, what might happen to me or a loved one, and the fear of getting lost or being alone. There are no words to explain how this all made me feel. At once I felt sick, lonely, and scared. I didn't want to be alone, ever.

I would stick to my mom like glue, wherever we went and if we were to go anywhere, I would get anxiety. Whether it was unfamiliar, or not, I was still scared of going places. What if I have to go to the bathroom? What if there is no bathroom? Then what? What if I get lost? What if I get kidnapped? What if I never see my family again? It was just what if, what if, what if! I was afraid of it all.

I was afraid of leaving my own home. What might happen to me or our house if I went out, even if it was only for a few minutes. I was afraid of change. I didn't want anything to change. Whether it was me growing up, or my parents getting a divorce, or going into a new grade. I wanted everything to stay the same.

So, if I could, I'd just stay in the comfort of my home, where I was used to it all. The noises, the furniture, and the comfort my bedroom brought to me. There, I was sure there would be no change.

If I didn't leave the house, I wouldn't be anxious. That was fine, right? Not at all. What I was experiencing, and still am, is agoraphobia.

CHAPTER 24:
THE TRUTH ABOUT AGORAPHOBIA

"So we can confidently say, 'The Lord is my helper; I will not fear; what can man do to me?'"

(Hebrews 13:6 ESV)

What happens when you get scared of being scared? Recently, I discovered that I have mild agoraphobia. It has gotten worse as I got older, but I am slowly working through it.

What is it like, you might wonder? Well, it's scary, very, very scary.

If there was a way I could stay in my lovable home forever I would. No anxiety-provoking situations to worry about. No mini heart attacks. But, sadly I cannot stay in my home forever. I have to get out and live. Have fun. You can't do that cooped up in a house all day. I'm not Rapunzel for goodness sake.

Going places is just complete torture for me, sometimes. All the worries circling my head and all the voices telling me terrible things; this makes me dread leaving my home. When I do go somewhere, I am okay for the most part, but the thought that maybe something could or will happen is overwhelming for me.

Sometimes, I hate crowds, sometimes I don't. Sometimes I'm in a grocery store aisle and I feel like there's no way out. Sometimes I can make it through a store without one worry.

With agoraphobia, there is a constant fear of being stuck somewhere, with no way out. You're afraid of leaving the house; going anywhere. My medication is helping with this, but of course, at times agoraphobia still occurs.

CHAPTER 25:
ANOTHER ATTACK

❧

"Sometimes the most important thing in a whole day is the rest taken between two deep breaths."

(Etty Hillesum)

I'm at the grocery store right now. The noises are just little things that most people could tolerate, but to me, they are huge, grubby monsters. I feel the anxiety overwhelm my body and start sweating; like the ocean is washing over me and it won't relent.

The sweat makes me feel hot and icky.

My whole body feels like it's on fire with me stuck inside, and somehow no matter what I do, I cannot seem to escape. My chest gets tighter and tighter with every breath until it's so squished I feel like I'm a bomb about to explode. Every gasp for air is a struggle. Every breath I draw in sends me deeper into the pit of worries.

I feel like I am drowning in this pit, and no matter what I do, I can't find my way back to the surface.

The pace of my heart quickens as I take another step down the aisle until it is beating so hard I can feel it pounding against my chest. My stomach is tight like my lungs, and it makes my stomach rumble. This pain aggravates until it's so unbearable that I completely lose reality. I find my way to the front of the store and sit down on a bench.

Taking deep breaths in, I try my best to calm my anxious mind. I sink into the seat and start listening to the lies in my mind. They say "I'm not good enough, and that everything is going wrong." No matter what I do I cannot seem to shut the voices out. They keep pressing, and they won't go away. I pray so hard begging for some control until the attack simmers down, and everything is okay again.

CHAPTER 26:
AMA'S P.O.V

"Challenges are what make life interesting, and overcoming them is what makes life meaningful."

(Joshua J. Marine)

My granddaughter is a joy to be around. She's a lively girl; really fun to be around. She's perky, and can never fail to make me laugh. When she's not suffering from anxiety, she can enjoy her life.

Right before a panic attack, Alivia gets quite agitated, shows fear towards easy things, and starts panicking. When she starts panicking she gets nervous and fearful. She starts lashing out over everything; not meaning to hurt anyone. She gets upset over little matters.

When she's having anxiety it prevents her from doing many things. She doesn't want to engage in activities that are supposed to be fun. She can't have a meaningful relationship with someone. She can't seem to enjoy life with anxiety steamrolling over the top of her.

Anxiety is not a happy thing; it's a sad thing. It's always being stressed, always being worried, always being afraid. You want to enjoy life as others do, but you don't know how to escape your anxious state. You feel like nobody understands, which can often lead to physical issues. This is why she was put on medication.

Before being prescribed medication Alivia was easily agitated, saddened, and annoyed. She was easily triggered into anger, making it hard to be around her at times. Alivia was always lashing out, hurting others on accident, or getting herself hurt.

Someone might say something to her, and she'd take it literally. If it was meant to be funny, she'd often take it the wrong way and get offended. Alivia wouldn't be as loving, she'd say mean things, and people would feel like they were constantly walking on eggshells. She was difficult to be around. Everyone wanted to help her, but we didn't know-how.

After she was put on medication, I immediately saw the sweet Alivia I know. She's so much easier to get along with and is more open-minded and daring. She's willing to try new things, and take chances she wouldn't have before. There was still a level of fear as well as anxiety, but a much lower level that wasn't nearly as extreme.

Now she's loving, and just overall happier. Alivia sees the good in life and can enjoy it again. She can play games with her family, without getting irritated. She has a sense of humor and can laugh freely. She's herself.

Alivia is currently at the stage where she's working through her disorders. She's taking her meds even when she doesn't want to. She is willingly going to therapy. She's getting the help she needs, avoiding stressful situations until she feels she's ready.

Alivia,

I believe if you continually pray and ask God for help and guidance you will be okay.

"Let your gentleness be evident to all. The Lord is near. Do not be anxious about anything, but in every situation, by prayer and petition, with thanksgiving, present your requests to God. And the peace of God, which transcends all understanding, will guard your hearts and your minds in Christ Jesus" (Philippians 4: 5-).

Ama

CHAPTER 27:
THE DECIDING FACTORS

"The first step towards change is awareness. The second step is acceptance."

(Nathaniel Branden)

When Alivia is not anxious she is very chill and enjoys the fun parts of life. She loves hanging out with friends, being outside, playing games, and running around wild and free.

When Alivia has a panic attack it often includes her smashing her head against me, squeezing my hand, and asking me to pray for her while she's hyperventilating deep breathing, or crying in anguish as if she's in pain. Her face looks white and her eyes red and puffy. She grabs her head as if she has a headache. She refuses to eat, gags when she tries to, and begs to stay home from school. There are a lot of tears. She has an expression of fear and panic written all over her face.

When an anxiety attack is on its way I notice her temper flares, she gets irritable and super angry. She begins feeling frustrated by everything. Her temper is short and she often cusses at me or others. That's when I started thinking about medication for her.

CHAPTER 28:
THE BENEFIT OF ANXIETY MEDICATION—MOM'S P.O.V

~

"Any change, even a change for the better, is always accompanied by drawbacks and discomfort"

(Arnold Bennett)

Before deciding to try anxiety meds she'd panic to the point of throwing up. Her stomach would be super crampy, and she'd panic. Alivia wouldn't want to leave my side, and she would be scared to go places outside of the home or traveling even to fun places. I had to force her (screaming) to go places.

Even though it hurt me to see her so upset, and not wanting to do things, as a mom I needed to push her. I needed to force her to get out of her comfort zone and try new things. I needed to show her that bad things don't always happen and that most of the time you usually can find joy or fun in trying something new. She used to think something bad would happen all the time, and she had to be by a bathroom at all times in case she'd get sick from her fear.

After Alivia got put on her medication, she began being more willing to try new things, go places, actually allowing herself to enjoy going places; not always in fear of what might happen. She didn't panic as much, and she just had simple morning anxiety before going off to school for the day. It was encouraging to see her able to travel more easily, without constant gagging, not eating, and stomach issues.

CHAPTER 29:
ANALISE'S P.O.V

⁓

"Everybody's a genius. But if you judge a fish by its ability to climb a tree, it will live its whole life believing that it is stupid."

(Albert Einstein)

Alivia's panic attacks often come out of nowhere. When she does have a panic attack she starts crying, having a meltdown, saying she's about to throw up, and then starts gagging. She begins to squirt peppermint in her mouth and cradle her stomach.

It's difficult to help her calm down. She usually does best when she is alone with her thoughts. When Alivia is experiencing a panic attack she screams at people and hates it whenever someone tries to help her.

Before being prescribed medicine she was always angry, always said she was going to kill herself and our family out of anger. Alivia experienced frequent shutdowns, and intense meltdowns. She wouldn't eat, she'd make herself sick, throw up a lot, and wouldn't want to leave the house. Her disorders prevent her from enjoying trips, school activities, enjoying meals, and being social.

After Alivia was prescribed medicine, everything became much milder. She's more relaxed, happier, and enjoyable to be around.

Alivia,

Living with you is a whole different story. It's difficult to talk to you because you take everything as something against you. You like to use your disorders as an excuse for your behavior. When you're in a good mood, you can be extremely fun to hang out with and be around. You can snap randomly and make people change their minds about hanging out with you, though.

I love you.

Analise

CHAPTER 30:
SAM'S P.O.V

~

"Ohana means family and family means nobody gets left behind or forgotten."

(Lilo and Stitch)

When Alivia is not anxious she's enjoyable to be around. I like playing with her, talking to her, and being around her.

My favorite activities to play with her are Legos; we spend hours building amazing houses for our Minifigures to live in. We also enjoy video games, especially the Show; we make our own World Series. Usually, I can convince her to play Pepper, ride scooters outside, or build stuff out of wood to climb on if she's in a decent mood.

She can be extremely rude sometimes, where nobody wants to play with her, and when she gets like this she can be a major cusser.

Sam

CHAPTER 31:
DAISY'S P.O.V

❧

"As you start to walk out on the way, the way appears."

(Rumi)

It's interesting living with my sister, Alivia. When she's not anxious she's usually pretty fun to be around. She's nice because she is willing to play with me, and make slime. When Alivia has a panic attack she sucks on peppermint candies, because her tummy hurts.

She isn't happy when she's experiencing anxiety. She doesn't like going to school, or doing any form of traveling, because she's afraid of the unknown. When she's having anxiety, she tends to pet our kittens, squeeze fidget toys, draw, and breathe (really deeply).

I think my sister can overcome it by playing with slime, or other fidget toys.

Alivia,

I just want to tell you that you're the best at making slime.

P.S. She poops for two hours.

Daisy

CHAPTER 32: FAMILY

───── ∿ ─────

"Being a family means you are a part of something very wonderful. It means you will love and be loved for the rest of your life."

(Lisa Weed)

Being part of my family is the best thing that ever happened to me. Do you want to know why? It's because they're kind to me even when I'm a jerk to them. It's because they care about me, even when I could care less about them. It's because they're always there for me no matter what; even when I'm doing my own thing and not paying any attention to them or their needs.

My family has helped me and supported me in numerous ways throughout the years. They never fail to make me smile with a funny YouTube video, or a stupid little joke. They allow me to follow my dreams and that's how I am here today, sharing my story with my readers. I've wanted to publish a book since I was 8 years old, and now here I am thanks to my extremely supportive family and friends. They have been a huge help during and after my diagnosis, by encouraging me to keep going and be strong.

My mom has done so much to help me cope with my disorders. First, she made sure she had me tested to get the correct diagnosis. Then, she sought out help for me by getting a counselor that I could trust and talk to. She even made sure I was put on medication for my anxiety and depression, because that is what was best for me.

My grandparents have been helpful as well, in so many wonderful ways. They have always been there for me and they always try their best to make me feel comfortable. When I was younger, I used to be afraid to go to anyone's house, even my own grandparents. They made sure I felt safe there and now I have no problem going. Whenever we go on a trip to the beach, Disneyland, etc, my Pa drives his RV so that I have a bathroom with me the whole time. I am beyond thankful for them and all the sacrifices they have made to help me feel less anxious.

Then, my siblings, who have never failed to make me laugh when I'm having a bad day. They always try to include me in things, whether it's a game or something else; they always work on including me in things even though I'm different. They know I'm different from them, and that I don't always understand concepts right away, but they rarely care. They always try to explain things to me by breaking it down to help me to understand things better.

I am blessed to have such a wonderful family. Thank you to my Mom, Ama, Pa, Analise, Samuel, and Daisy for being so patient with me!

CHAPTER 33:
THE ABILITY TO BREATHE

"If you want to conquer the anxiety of life, live in the moment, live in the breath."

(Amit Ray)

My mom has always been the one to push me towards my goals. She's made me tough through my diagnosis, suffering, and other hard events in my life. She has taught me not to look at it as a disadvantage, but instead something different about myself.

She's made me try so hard sometimes, and so much that I hurt inside from my exhaustion. She has to be hard on me, so that I realize how much I need to move forward with this, and believe in myself.

She's taught me to train myself to stop my attacks, and overcome my anxiety. Because of this, I am who I am now, and I am a tough girl who is continually trying and training for the bigger events to come.

My mom made me who I am today, and all I can say is thank you Mom for believing in me all this time. For giving me the ability to finally breathe.

EPILOGUE

❧

*"Don't dilute yourself for any person or any reason. You are
enough! Be unapologetically you."*

(Steve Maraboli)

Sometimes I wish it would all just go away. The disorders, the anxiety, the depression. I've been through so much, good and bad. I realize that these things are part of who I am, and I've learned to accept this because God created me specifically, and He doesn't make mistakes.

Every time I have a rough day, I think of how far I've come, and how God is always there for me when I need him the most. He listens no matter the day. He loves me.

I've tried to look beyond my disorders and live a normal life, but I've realized there is no such thing as normal. Throughout my anxiety and depression diagnoses I realized that they are a part of me. They contribute to who I am. Even though they are not my definition of beautiful, they do shape me into a better person in God's eyes, and he loves me for who I am.

Every human being is different and extraordinary in their own beautiful way. We shouldn't have to feel like we need to change ourselves to be loved. We are how we are and we are beautiful in God's eyes.

Don't let anxiety or any other disorders you may have get in the way of life.

You are amazing, never forget that.

You are loved, always remember that.

You are the boss, not anxiety.

You own you, not anxiety.

You have the right to kick anxiety out, and never let it back in.

All you have to do is be strong, and believe in yourself.

I love you, I believe in you, I think you're amazing, and you can do anything if you just believe.

Thank you to all of those who have bought this book. You are not only listening to what I have to say about anxiety, but you're helping a girl pursue her dreams in writing. I hope you found comfort in what I've shared.

Thank you all so, so much!

Alivia Jones

ENCOURAGING BIBLE VERSES

Proverbs 3: 5-6

"Trust in the Lord with all thine heart, and lean not unto thine

own understanding.

In all thy ways acknowledge him, and he shall direct thy

paths."

Philippians 4: 13

"I can do all things through him who gives me strength."

Matthew 6: 34

"Therefore do not be anxious about tomorrow, for tomorrow will be anxious for itself. Sufficient for the day is its own trouble."

Isaiah 35: 4

"Say to those with fearful hearts, "Be strong, do not fear; your God will come, he will come with vengeance; with divine retribution, he will come to save you."

Joshua 1: 9

"Have I not commanded you? Be strong and courageous. Do not be afraid; do not be discouraged, for the LORD your God will be with you wherever you go."

Psalm 94: 19

"When anxiety was great within me, your consolation brought me joy."

Deuteronomy 31: 8

"The Lord himself goes before you and will be with you; he will never leave you nor forsake you. Do not be afraid; do not be discouraged."

Psalm 23: 4

"Even though I walk through the valley of the shadow of death, I will fear no evil, for you are with me; your rod and your staff, they comfort me."

Matthew 6: 33

"But seek first the kingdom of God and his righteousness, and all these things will be added to you."

Psalm 40: 1-2

"I waited patiently for the Lord; he inclined to me and heard my cry. He drew me up from the pit of destruction, out of the miry bog, and set my feet upon a rock, making my steps secure."

Psalm 34: 18

"The Lord is near to the brokenhearted and saves the crushed in spirit."

ABOUT THE AUTHOR

A livia Jones wrote her memoir—Breathe— to share her journey of what it is like living with anxiety, depression, and high-functioning Aspergers. She's a strong Christian who believes that God has big plans for her. Alivia enjoys writing, drawing, crafting, swimming, fishing, and hanging out with friends. She lives in California with her amazing mom, two beautiful sisters, and her awesome brother.